Salvat-Papasseit: Selected poems

Joan Salvat-Papasseit
SELECTED POEMS

Catalan text with translations and Introduction

by

DOMINIC KEOWN

and

TOM OWEN

1982

THE ANGLO-CATALAN SOCIETY

THE ANGLO-CATALAN SOCIETY
OCCASIONAL PUBLICATIONS

© *Poems. Heirs of Joan Salvat-Papasseit*
© *Introduction and Translations. Dominic Keown and Tom Owen*

Printed by Parchment (Oxford) Ltd.
Design by Joan Gili

ISSN No. 0144-5863
ISBN No. 0 9507137 1 6

CONTENTS

INTRODUCTION

For Sammy and Ceris
and to the memory of Pete Sowerby

The Present Translation of Salvat-Papasseit

The intention of the Anglo-Catalan Society's occasional publications is to bring to a specialist and wider interested public aspects of Catalan social and cultural life. This first translation of selected poems by Salvat-Papasseit into the English language is seen by the translators as a contribution to this aim and as a privileged opportunity to make the work of this remarkable poet available to an English speaking audience and to place him in the centre of European modernist achievement.

Our realization that it was possible to translate Salvat's poems in terms of a substantial body of work rather than as a few occasional or anthology pieces, was initially a gradual one. (The view was at one time that he was virtually untranslatable into English.) For those new to the poetry of Salvat-Papasseit an account of our encounter through translation may help to focus attention on some of the unique characteristics of this author. One of the translators (D.K.) has been familiar with the poet's work for a number of years as a researcher and the other (T.O.) came fresh to Salvat as a poet and a translator. We have attempted to capitalize on this particular mix of talents and perspectives and certainly we have found the experience a rewarding one which we hope to share with a new readership.

There is a considerable body of literature devoted to the art of translation and we do not want to burden the reader with some of the many controversies surrounding the subject. However, one thing is clear to us: the translator/poet is often forced to dwell closely on the key linguistic and stylistic devices of a poet, a fact which can often afford a fresh if not privileged insight.

Our first working encounter with Salvat was with that dense, angular poem "The Absurd" and the feverish and strangely haunting "Milady Death". These would have provided an excellent anthology selection for any poetry magazine. The "Nocturn for Accordion" was so impressive for us that we decided to proceed to a much more comprehensive selection of translations. This masterly poem which unfolds with its bitter railing and wounded sense of being misunderstood is crowned by that remarkable, moving and elegant vision of impoverished street children of the Barcelona dockland, in the circle of the night-watchman's fire with their "hands meeting like a farandola".

For us Salvat is a poet who generates empathy for a number of other reasons. Like the translators', his formative creative periods are nurtured by an urban and industrial environment. It is this style of life that he constantly celebrates. His libertarian, socialist and national inclinations are still for us relevant and central impulses in the present European political, social and cultural crisis.

Salvat was one of the small group of Catalan poets to fall under the early influence of the Italian Futurists, and he shares with them and the Russian Futurists that fascination with innovation, movement and the dynamism of city life. It is intriguing for us to note how each of these "national" futurist tendencies developed its own specific relationship between cultural radicalism and differing kinds of political commitments. All three had a nationalist ingredient: however, it was only Italian Futurism which affiliated itself to the despairing radicalism of Fascism. There are other parallels. It is not surprising that the fascination with urban dynamism grips a small plebeian bohemia located on a rapidly expanding industrial and commercial centre, surrounded by the general torpidity of social relations in the whole of the Peninsula.

What we find remarkable in the work of Salvat-Papasseit is that the heritage of Futurist activism works through in a more oblique and distanced fashion. Although his crippling health problems, which led to his premature death, would have concentrated his sense of distance from social events, it seems to us that his poems of yearning and nostalgia, his desire for an "active" occupation represent far more than the wishful meanderings of a consumptive minor poet. Although the moods of his poems vacillate from confident optimism through ambivalence to dark despair, the city as subject is constant; its ebb and flow, its plebeian population and its vitality are a counterpointing motif.

This immanent sense of movement and response to the activity of urban life mark out Salvat's poetry and indeed would baffle those readers who would expect or would seek out the tendentious voice or message. The response to what Mayakovsky called the "social command"[1] is located rather in the construction of the events of everyday life than in a reading of prescriptive exhortations. This perception of Salvat's work is forced on the reader/translator and we were made particularly aware of it in confronting the extreme complexities of the temporal and modal structures of the verb, which for us is a pivotal component in his poetry. Salvat probably makes more use of the conditional tense and subjunctive mood than any of the poets we have encountered. There are poems of yearning "If I were a fisherman...", etc., which draw on a tradition of naive or folkloric mythology of popular heroes. Bohemian braggadocio and populist mythologizing often combine during the volatile periods of the social formation of oppressed peoples. And indeed in a superficial reading Salvat appears to conform to that stereotype of the semi-lumpen proletarian mentality; an almost ecstatic revolt vitiated by periods of despairing acceptance or contemplative withdrawal. A closer reading of his texts, we would argue, reveals a far more complex manipulation of verbal modalities. For example in the poem "Give me a Saint" the original imperative is followed by a series of conditionals, but the final stanza switches to an indicative and "simple" statement of immanence, then back to conditionality:

Jo hi *aniria* de matí, en 'quella hora
en què *deixo* l'amiga abans no *surti* el sol,
quan a l'església *obririen* la porta:

—*duria* l'estampeta arran, arran del cor.

In this example of temporal and modal switching we begin to discern that "ontological" shift which is so characteristic of the

1.   V. Mayakovsky, *How Verses are Made*, translated by E. M. Hyde (London 1970), p. 18.

modernist enterprise. What is interesting and hopeful for us in the case of Salvat-Papasseit is that we do not experience a collapse into stylized Romantic anguish and gloom. What we perceive is a progress towards a legitimate voluntarism constantly desiring to make a utopia of every moment of life.

This kind of structural reading of Salvat's devices has afforded us an opportunity to assess the status of the "choir" of plebeian archetypes who populate his poems: the "Love Vendor", the gamblers, the night-watchmen, the girls on trams, etc., the street people. The awareness of these "figures" does not have the common sense "solidity" of being, of assumed permanence of the stereotypes of popular wisdom. Because of their projection, they have far more in common with the multi-faceted angularity of Cubist semi-figurative "still-life". Salvat's concern with the oppositions of temporal and modal sequences may explain some of his strategies for dealing with temporal and physical location. For example, the later poem "Nostalgia for Tomorrow", a celebration of the domestic and familiar, presents us with a central ambivalence, through the opposition of possibilities encompassed by the definite and almost putative perception of continuity. The poet's speculative handling of a domestic ritual between friends leaves us with a sense of fragility that rescues this poem from its alleged sentimentalism.

For us the most notable poem of this type is "Nothing is Paltry". Here the poet has discarded the speculative dimension to hammer out a series of assertions through the indicative mood. The poem is a statement of the "totality" of things. Apart from the repeated negative, "nothing is paltry", the poem is a sequence of axioms which not only celebrate the richness and multi-faceted interconnection of things but also give expression to the will to transcend change and dissolution. The predicate nouns have now a qualitatively different status to those under the governance of conditionality; the naming of things offers the poet the practice of constant renewal; a contemporary Russian Cubo-Futurist poet Kruchenykh encapsulates the spirit of this kind of voluntarist nominalism:

Words die, the world stays young for ever. An artist has seen the world in a new way, and like Adam, he gives his own names to everything.[2]

It would not be proper for us to leave the impression that there were no difficulties encountered in this translation. Each language has its unique set of expressive possibilities. Our task was made more problematic because of a number of other factors. Salvat often deals simultaneously with demotic and literary registers, a literary practice which offers a multiplicity of referents through word association and punning, etc.. Fortunately the English language affords us the flexibility of our separate Latin and "Anglo-Saxon" origins which also sometimes strongly mark out the social discrepancies in language usage.

The next set of problems arises from the "modernist" mode. Some of Salvat's work exhibits extreme levels of semantic and syntactical dislocation. In cases of this kind we have attempted to keep as close as possible to the Catalan text to presence the original impact. Similarly we were aware that Salvat was often attempting highly complex forms of modal and semantic patterning through a vehicle which still retains the characteristic inaccuracies of popular speech. Where feasible, we have registered as accurately as possible Salvat's own preferences.

The other difficulties we encountered were in the domain of sexual politics. We resisted the pressure of censorship by exclusion of poems which may be read by some as "sexist". Sexual politics of the early 20th-century libertarian and socialist movements have a different "historic" determination from ours. We are aware that Salvat's perception of sexual liberation can be read as almost exclusively male-centred and we note the limitations of this perception. In this respect our inclusion of "Love Vendor" might appear to be controversial. For us it is not legitimate to censure a poet for the statements or projections of personae. We read this poem as a disturbingly ambiguous portrayal of the enticements and boasting of the city pimp as a sinister metaphor for "respectable" or "romantic" sexual appropriation.

2.   Alexei Kruchenykh, "Declaration of the word as such", quoted by Vladimir Markov in *Russian Futurism (London 1969), pp. 130-131.*

In these brief notes on our encounter as translators of Salvat-Papasseit we have attempted to share some of our excitement and our appreciation of this tragic and triumphant poet. Like many of his generation, their lives and work appeared to have been extinguished by the dark night of Fascist nihilism. We hope that our work will contribute in a small way to restoring to Salvat the proper European perspective on his rightfully important place in Catalan literature.

The Poet

Joan Salvat-Papasseit was born in Barcelona in May 1894. In 1901 his father, a merchant sailor, died in mysterious circumstances at sea, which meant even harder times for the impoverished family. The next five years were spent in the dock poorhouse and, apart from a series of recuperative stays in sanatoria in later life, the port environment was to provide the poet's only permanent home.

By 1907 Salvat-Papasseit had embarked upon an extended career of casual labour, employed in capacities as diverse as apprentice statue-maker, grocer's boy and, later, night-watchman on the docks. His late teens heralded the start of a lifelong acquaintance with political and literary groups. In 1914 he became a member of the *Juventud Socialista de Barcelona* and joined the editorial staff of the progressive social journal *Los Miserables.*

Self-taught and largely ignorant of the philosophy of dialectics, Salvat's revolutionary zeal stemmed from a sense of sheer indignation and horror at contemporary social injustice. Sentenced to two months' imprisonment in 1916 for his political writings, his first collection of articles *Glosas de un socialista* was published the same year under the pseudonym Gorkiano.

The publication of *Humo de fábrica* in 1918 marks the end of the first phase of politico-literary activity. Salvat had at last found suitable employment as manager of the book section of "Galeries Laietanes", and his work becomes much more intimate and lyrical in inspiration. Castilian prose is superseded by poetry in the maternal language of Catalan. Doctrinaire socialism gives way to a more nebulous libertarianism with a corresponding greater aesthetic concern, as evinced by the launching of various artistic reviews.

In July 1918 Salvat married Carme Eleuterio and it was around this time that the first severe symptoms of tuberculosis appeared — the illness which was to bring about his premature death.

The last years of Salvat's life comprised an intense literary activity and long stays in sanatoria at the expense of various wealthy benefactors. The medical treatment, however, proved ineffectual and was unable to halt the spread of the disease. The poet's physical resistance faded and the last days of his life were spent in great physical agony. Salvat-Papasseit died on the 7th of August 1924 and was buried the following day in the *Cementiri del Sud-oest* in Barcelona.

The collections of poems from which the main body of this anthology is taken were all published during the period 1919-24. The poems which make up ÓSSA MENOR/*URSA MINOR* — released posthumously in 1925 — were found hidden under the pillow of Salvat's deathbed.

The Poetry

The early poetry of Salvat reflects the influence of two major artistic currents. Catalan *Modernisme* of the late nineteenth century was a movement which aspired to create for Catalonia a *modern*, cosmopolitan and authentically *national* culture. Its most successful poet, Joan Maragall (1860-1911), had given voice to the basic Nietzschean preoccupations about the individual and society. In terms of this theme and its expression Salvat echoes the basic concern of his poetical predecessor.

The formative years of Salvat's literary awareness coincided with the arrival in Catalonia of the innovatory mode of the Avant-garde. It is not surprising that the movement should have found such a positive response from this nation. The social problems of the Principality mirrored those of modern Europe, both in labour's challenge to capital and the growth of national consciousness and desire for autonomy and unity by various ethnic groups. It was against such a backcloth that this artistic mode had first appeared years earlier elsewhere on the continent. The mood of contemporary Catalonia, then, was suitable for its immediate assimilation.

The title of the first collection POEMES EN ONDES HERTZIANES/*POEMS IN HERTZIAN WAVES* (1919) illustrates the impact of Italian Futurism on the young poet with its characteristic eulogy of the machine age. The "Letter from Italy" reveals certain other traits typical of this school: overt *anti-passatismo* and an emphasis on dynamism enhanced stylistically by the disjointed syntax and non-causal action. We include it here as overture to our anthology, in the same way as it prefaced Salvat's first volume, with the necessary reminder that the vagueness of many of its references constitutes an essential part of its original impact.

Nonetheless the "Memory of a 'Fugue' by Bach" from the same collection, shows that Salvat would not content himself with mere regurgitation of Futurist commonplaces. The reference to the circus and the attempted elimination of barriers between art forms — in this case music and verse — are essentially Vanguard in inspiration and reflect the influence of this trend.

However, the poem is delicate, imaginative, and, moreover, restrained. The rambling flights of fantasy capture the tone of many of Bach's fugues. Surprisingly the controversial overwhelming power in expression is absent here, which suggests a propensity in Salvat to be selective in terms of style and theme, and a reticence to be governed by any rigid adherence to Futurist doctrine. Indeed this is one of the features of Salvat's creative process; a continuous adapting, remoulding and re-articulation of topics to comply with his own particular poetic sensitivities.

This phenomenon is apparent in the second collection, L'IRRADIADOR DEL PORT I LES GAVINES/*THE PORT BEACON AND THE SEA-GULLS* (1921). The Futurist leaning is still evident in "Battle Song". The artist is isolated and antagonistic towards the Establishment. "The Absurd" reveals the mystery and wonder peculiar to the Vanguardist vision of the world. Banality, routine and drudgery are completely absent, with the emphasis falling firmly on vitality and adventure, as everyday reality is transformed into something startling and new.

Salvat nonetheless was ever the poet of his own ethos, and evocative accounts of daily scenes of urban life pervade his work. "Still on the Tram" and "Christmas" provide suitable examples of this. Technically they are not the most accomplished of his poems, but they rank among the most popular on account of the warm human response they provoke.

It is in this collection that Salvat first formulates his basic poetic stance and expresses it with any real force and coherence. "Wedding March", "Nostalgia for Tomorrow" and "Nothing is Paltry" are crucial in this respect and form the thematic backbone of the work as a whole.

"Nothing is Paltry" is a straightforward statement of the poet's vision, though its sheer power belies a good deal of complexity in expression. All creation shares the same underlying essence, "the song sings in every flake of things", and enjoys an inherent promise of futurity, "and every leaf ever green". Death may occur on an individual level but the life-cycle is eternal and it is this assurance of continuance on the general scale which accounts for the poet's exuberance:

— Avui demà i ahir	— *Today, tomorrow and yesterday*
s'esfullarà una rosa:	*a rose will wither:*
i a la verge més jove li	*and to the youngest virgin's*
vindrà llet al pit.	*breast comes milk.*

The fusion of the three time scales controlled by the verb in the future tense underlines this point most emphatically. The reference to the fecundation of the young virgin is purely symbolic. The continuance of the reproductive cycle is crystallised in the image of the perennial journey of the youngest girl to motherhood, which again reflects the basic theme.

"Nostalgia for Tomorrow" transposes this same vision of life onto a typical everyday scene. It has been correctly regarded as one of Salvat's finest poems but has for long been interpreted as no more than a nostalgic evocation of urban life by a man isolated from his environment and close to death. There is, however, far too much control and intricacy in the actual construction of the poem to suggest that it is merely a simple exercise in sentimentality.

The description of the scene is achieved through a whole host of technical devices: polysyndeton, pleonasm, metaphor, zeugma, typographical detail, etc.. These are coupled with a carefully conceived structural progression and time sequence: exterior to interior; dawn time quietude to morning animation to afternoon restfulness, all succesfully evoked through change in rhythm and pace.

However, it is the intensity of the last four lines which explains this detail and precision as the drift of the poem is lifted from the bounds of banality to reiterate the basic message of "Nothing is Paltry". The capitals underline this change:

> — Vosaltres restareu,   — *You will remain,*
> per veure el bo que és tot: *to see how good it all is:*
> i la Vida   *Life and*
> i la Mort.   *Death.*

Salvat looks upon the life-cycle "Life and Death" yet realises its permanence and continuity in the general sense, "You will remain". It is this insight which explains the joy the poet feels when confronted with existence, "how good it all is".

The first half of the poem gives us the particular example of this with the technical precision suggesting meaning which extends beyond the everyday. The second part of the poem relates the full relevance of these trivial events to the totality of the life-cycle, lifting the poem far beyond the realm of sentimentality. It is a further example of Salvat's poetic insight as the poet intuits the general and universal in the individual and anecdotal.

"Wedding March" also reveals Salvat's technical prowess, especially his ability to adapt and rework innovatory modes to convey his own very particular and personal vision. The calligram comprises three distinct sections. The first presents a solitary clown figure amid the total confusion of some grotesque circus ring. Salvat's figure looks at the world from a standpoint of sheer egocentricity: "The earth only turns because I am here". He is not concerned with others, only himself, "Margot...Only burns for me". However this self-centred stance can only bring anguish and death, "I am a BUFFOON who is dying", as is exemplified by the fall from the trapeze.

A solution to this solitude and absurdity is attempted in the second part along the lines of the basic Vanguard criteria of dynamism, "LIFE for Dynamism", and antagonism, "Gob on the shaved dome of the cretins". However this also proves unsatisfactory, "I protest that this may also degenerate". Confusion still remains as the lion-tamer inexplicably "wants to juggle".

At this point, the poem changes in direction. Vitality returns, but in a positive sense, with a reference to Eddison. The negative clown figure of the first part is replaced by the affirmative qualities of the much admired Chaplin. The answer to the anguish of solitude and death is now at hand and is expressed — as in "Nothing is Paltry" — through the motif of sex. The sexual act, with the notion of reproduction, becomes symbolic of the repeated life-round. Sex is expressed in terms of time in the figure of a clock. This constitutes a fusion of the temporal and natural cycles, which underlines the perennial nature of existence: "The Orb of the clock at TWELVE spawns the hours to come". Just as time will continue so too will life, and it is the poet's realization of this fact, together with his participation in the process, which assures him of some sense of immortality: "and so I will be immortal as from now has been born/my I in the ALL".

It is this more abstract and conceptual line that Salvat's poetry follows as everyday reality is transformed through the eyes of the poet to display facets of a much deeper universal quality. Similarly the topic of sex is amplified to encompass the expression of two basic ideas. On a personal level it is evocative of the pleasure, beauty and excitement of life. Moreover it will retain this general symbolic aspect of representing the continuation of the life-cycle. It is these two elements which form the basic thematic structure of EL POEMA DE LA ROSA ALS LLAVIS/*POEM OF THE ROSE IN THE LIPS*.

This work has been considered one of the finest erotic poems in the Catalan language, though its meaning clearly extends beyond the level of mere physical stimulation. Although in the form of a collection, it is basically one poem which follows a clear pattern of development. "I will Leave the City" shows the poet resolving to devote his whole attention to this topic. "And the Wind Left", "Under my Lips, Hers", "Since she is Tall and Fine", display the sheer joy of sex. "And when the Confiding Trees" reiterates the connexion between the particular and general levels of meaning.

The collection ends quite appropriately in an anti-climax. A specific *affaire* has finished, "If You Went Away", though it has lasting significance in view of its symbolic value. The poet will encounter this woman and all that she symbolises in his journey through life.

These topics are also apparent in LA GESTA DELS ESTELS/*THE EXPLOITS OF THE STARS* and ÓSSA MENOR/*URSA MINOR.* In the "Devices" the sexual question is linked with an element of antagonism: "The star of a glance/the flash of a flag./War and love;/salt and earth". Gone, however, is the gratuitous aggression of "Wedding March". The fight has now become more essential, and the fusion of these two elements implies that along with the continuation of life, struggle in the most general sense is one of the main attributes of existence. We are correspondingly urged not to avoid it, "believe in war because it is good to struggle".

"Give me a Saint" is an illustration of one of the major developments in the later work with regard to the question of religion. It is an emphatic rejection of orthodox Christianity as Salvat's patron possesses none of the conventional saintly qualities: "That saint ever a beautiful girl;/...so pure, white, fresh and young/like the cream of lambs-wool...". She has all the earthy immediacy of a fertility goddess.

This distinct pagan flavour is also evident in the evocation of various rituals throughout the later work. There are a significant number of poems describing the celebration of Michaelmas, Pentecost, Easter, etc., and what they signify ties in very closely with the basic message:

> ... in the seasonal festivities this motive is particularly apparent... The wonderful cycle of the year, with its hardships and periods of joy, is celebrated and delineated, and represented as continued in the life-round of the human group.[3]

The evocation of seasonal festivities, then, with their celebration of the continued life-round, is quite appropriate. More particularly impressive, however, is the transformation of everyday urban scenes into rituals, which thereby imbues them with the same importance as the pagan festivities. "Take a Walk through the Port" is a fine example of this wherein Barcelona docks become the setting for some type of fertility rite, "a pagan feast", complete with a suitable orgiastic element — "the drunken sailors gazed upon her/and bought drinks for all the passers-by".

A similar enacting of ritual occurs in the market place in "By the Market", where the anecdotal level is given a wider general relevance by the very structure of the poem. The individual events of the stanzas become united to the general impersonal whole, conveyed in the refrain "here's how the neighbours chew the rag". The repeated chorus underlines the recurrence of this phenomenon. Once again Salvat adapts his material well. The significance of ritual is transposed onto the urban location to reiterate the basic message.

> ...The whole society becomes visible to itself as an impersonal living unit. Generations of individuals pass, like anonymous cells from a living body, but the sustaining, timeless form remains.[4]

Stylistically, this shows a marked progession from the handling of the same theme in "Nostalgia for Tomorrow".

The most successful example of this process, however, is "Nocturn for Accordion", which recalls Salvat's time as a night-watchman in the port. Here the dockland is transformed into the setting for some mystical quasi-religious ceremony. The reader is kept in ignorance of what is actually transpiring, "You don't know/what it is/to watch wood on the wharf", which increases the mood of mystery, as the poet, an initiated priest-like figure,

3.   J. Campbell, *The Hero with a Thousand Faces* (Princeton 1949), p. 384.
4.   *Ibid*, p. 383.

officiates over some primeval ceremony, "but all the hands of all the street kids/met like a farandola/to swear an oath in the ring of my fire./And it was like a miracle/drawing out their stiff numb hands."

The implication is apparent. In his reconstruction of everyday reality, Salvat removes the veneer of banality from typical scenes of urban life to reveal a force of a more general and permanent nature.

It has been suggested that this evocation of ritual was the attempt of an isolated consumptive to escape from the dreadful limitations imposed by ill-health, and somehow commune with his beloved urban environment. To see things in this way is to miss much of the technical expertise and symbolic force of Salvat's mature poetic work.

ACKNOWLEDGEMENTS

The translators would like to express their gratitude to Omnium Cultural and to the Instituto de España in London for their financial assistance to the Anglo-Catalan Society's Occasional Publications. We are also indebted to the Yorkshire Arts Council for their encouragement.

The text of the Catalan poems is reproduced by kind permission of Edicions Ariel, Barcelona, publishers of Salvat-Papasseit's complete poems in the series Clàssics Catalans Ariel, edited by Joaquim Molas.

Our thanks also to Joan Gili and Alan Yates for their editorial and literary guidance, and to Sandie Murphy, Audrey Stapley and Sally-Anne Pye for their patient and skilful contribution in preparing copy for the printer.

POEMS

LLETRA D'ITALIA

Amic Millàs-Raurell:

Prampolini ha fet trossos la munífica vesta de Beatriu (de Giovanni-Duprè). Siena s'és commoguda. A Florència —per via sense fils— la dissort hi és vinguda així mateix: els plecs del monument a Ferrari Corbelli són desapareguts. Les pubilles, tot nues, s'han posat a cantar com diablesses una cançó infernal. Suara he arribat jo.

A «Valori Plastici», es diu: Giovanni Papini ha enviat per correu a Marx Bekman, un xop cervesa Pilsen. (Il mio futurismo.) — Ara no ho féssiu córrer, que els de «Noi» no s'ho poden acabar.

Aquí a Roma es murmura que per a comprendre En Foix de Sarrià hom deu llegir a Sófocles primer. La Laieta ha plorat, car haurà de tornar a començar pel Narro... perquè no el sap llegir.

Didac Ruiz, a Mòdena (ens ho ha fet saber Antonino Foschini), ha escrit que la blasfèmia és la rosa de foc de la virtut. Per aquest expedient Prampolini ha sortit de la presó.

—M· Giobbe ha esgrafiat una testa de Ruiz. —Giuseppe Ravegnani ha manat a Strawinsky que en fes la partitura: ha comprat els pentagrames a Gerald de Tyrwitt. Tot això no està bé, ja ho saps, però jo en enterar-me'n he enviat un telegrama a En V. Solé de Sojo. Que en tregui ell l'entrellat.

—En Carrà i En Soffici s'han canviat una tela. Es la darrera nova que he sabut.

/· J. Pellicer- Papasseit

LETTER FROM ITALY

My dear Millàs-Raurell:

Prampolini has ripped to shreds the munificent habit of Beatrice (by Giovanni-Duprè). Siena is shocked. In Florence — by wireless — misfortune has arrived in the same way: the pleats on the monument to Ferrari Corbelli have disappeared. The eldest daughters, stark naked, have started to sing like she-devils, a hellish song. This is where I came in.

At "Valori Plastici", it is said: Giovanni Papini has posted a jar of Pilsen beer to Marx Bekman, (Il mio futurismo). — Now don't spread it around, but the "Noi" lot just can't get over it.

Here in Rome the word is that to understand Foix from Sarrià you must read Sophocles first. Laieta cried because she'll have to go back to her ABC... since she can't read him.

Didac Ruiz, in Modena (this was made known to us by Antonino Foschini), has written that blasphemy is the fire-rose of virtue. Through this expedient Prampolini has got out of prison.

— M. Giobbe has adorned a head of Ruiz with graffiti. Guiseppe Ravegnani has ordered Stravinsky to write the score: he's bought the pentagrams from Gerald de Tyrwitt. All that isn't right, as you know, but when I found out I sent a telegram to V. Solé de Sojo. Let him sort it all out.

— Carrà and Soffici have swapped a canvas. That's the latest I've heard.

J. Salvat-Papasseit

EL RECORD D'UNA «FUGA» DE BACH

A J. M. Junoy

M'he esquitxat a Garraf

    he passat tretze porxos foradants de muntanya

només per veure a Sitges un blau brunzent de cuina i un blanc de calç lluent

                                        de celobert

On irà l'esquirol quan no trobi pinyons

         —mossegarà sa cua que en té el gust

Suara he fet una grua

        d'un full del calendari

        i ha baixat amb el número mateix

Almenys del Ministeri m'han avançat una hora de rellotge

Aquí on tot valor universal duu per nom Montjuïc

la lluna

la bruna

vestida

de dol

és més vídua i més clara

[24]

MEMORY OF A 'FUGUE' BY BACH

For J.M. Junoy

I slipped away to Garraf
                    passing the thirteen pierced porches in the mountain
only to see in Sitges a humming kitchen blue and a white of shining lime
                                    in a splash of sky

Where will the squirrel go when he can find no cones
                    — he'll chew his tail which tastes of pine

Now I've made a kite
                    from the leaf of a calendar
                    and it came down with the same number
          At least the Ministry have put my watch an hour forward
*Here where all universal value carries the name of Montjuïc**

               "The moon
               dark grey
               dressed
               *in mourning"***

                                    is more a widow and brighter

---

*   *Montjuïc* — a castle overlooking Barcelona. A prison and interrogation centre during
      social unrest over the turn of the century.

**   Refrain of a popular song.

Tot això un antiquari no ho sabria comprendre

He vist més: —Que l'infant de bolquers
                                        esguardava rient una estrella
Però cap llibre no parla del somrís de l'infant

I heus aquí que vaig dir-los   una cosa vulgar:
—L'estel hexagonal de colors en el Circ enclou totes les síntesis del món.

CANTO LA LLUITA

Cavaller d'un corser
                    qual crinera és de flames
só jo l'incendiari de mots d'adolescent
Blasmo els déus a ple vol:
                    l'arraulit bestiari
                                        tem el fuet del meu cant!
I he maridat la lluna...
(Però no dormo amb Ella si el filisteu governa els meus
                                                        domenys.)

All this an antiquary could not understand

I've seen more: — The child in swaddling clothes
                                                            looked up laughing at a star

    But no book talks of the smile of the child

And here's what I told them   something common:

— The hexagonal colour star in the Circus includes all the syntheses in the
                                                                                    world.

BATTLE SONG

Rider on a courser
                            whose mane is aflame
I am the incendiary of the words of adolescence
I curse the gods in full flight:
                            the quivering bestiary
                                        cringes at the whip of my song!
And I have married the moon...

(But I do not sleep with Her if the philistine rules my domain.)

L'ABSURD

El dau d'ivori
virolet de la sort i la malastrugança
i la poma al caliu que esbufega
com més corre el ventall

Els ulls miren els ulls
i la paraula és morta:
el pigat de les xifres parlarà

(Damunt la taula el vas
i la pàl·lida imatge de l'absenta)

I el meu company i jo
de suara perjurats a jugar-nos la vida amb el misteri:
TOTS 2 AL MATEIX NÚMERO DEL DAU

THE ABSURD

The ivory die
pied with luck and misfortune
and the apple in the ash that gasps
the more the bellows heave

Eyes look to eyes
and the word is dead:
the pocks on the ciphers will speak

(On the table the glass
and the pallid image of absinthe)

My partner and I
sworn from now to gamble our lives on mystery:
THE 2 OF US ON THE SAME NUMBER OF THE DIE

ENCARA EL TRAM

A D. Carles

Noia del tram, tens l'esguard en el llibre
i el full s'irisa
        en veure's cobejat.
I el cobrador s'intriga si giraràs el full:
sols per veure't els ulls!

Que les cames se't veuen
                i la mitja és ben fina:
                i tot el tram ets tu.
Però els ulls no se't veuen.

I la teva mà és clara
que fa rosa el teu cos de tafetà vermell,
        i el teu mocadoret ha tornat de bugada.
Però els ulls no els sabem!

I si jo baixés ara? —Mai no et sabria els ulls...
Té! Ara ja he baixat!

STILL ON THE TRAM

For D. Carles

Girl on the tram you've got your eyes in a book
and the page blushes
                    on being envied.
And the conductor wonders if you'll turn the page:
just to see your eyes!

We can see your legs
                    and the stocking so sheer;
                    and all the tram is you.
But we can't see your eyes.

And your hand is bright
tinted by your body of red taffeta,
        and your handkerchief, back from the wash.
But we don't know your eyes!

And if I were to get off? — I'd never know your eyes...
Look now. I've got off!

MARXA NUPCIAL

Llum de l'**IRRADIADOR** camaleònic damunt
l'estrella del <u>Circ</u> encara hexagonal

Exit!   Exit!!   Exit!!!

CLOWNS equilàters   líders romàntics
Això és sa   i en les constel·lacions de quatre barrets
cònics

La terra només gira perquè jo sóc aquí i jo sóc un
PALLASSO qui agonitza

Margot amb el **MALLOT** i els cabells pintats
rojos sembla un ciri que cremi
Només crema per mi:
Davant dels cent centaures que fan faixa a la Pista
<u>DAURADA</u> D'EMOCIÓ

Margot ara m'esguarda fit a fit   i en caient del
Trapezi he llegit un <u>anunci</u> a la pantalla:

Escopiu a la closca
pelada
dels cretins

Flash from the FLOODLIGHT chameleonic above the hexagonal
Circus star

        Roll up!   Roll up!!   Roll up!!!

CLOWNS equilaterals   romantic leaders
That's sound   and in the constellations of four conical
hats

The earth only turns because I am here and I am a
BUFFOON who is dying

Margot with her COSTUME and painted red hair looks like a
candle that burns
She only burns for me:
Before the hundred centaurs which girdle the Ring
GOLDEN WITH EXCITEMENT

Margot gazes at me eye to eye   and falling from
the Trapeze I read an advert on the screen:

Gob on the shaved
dome
    of the cretins

Aquest home que diu:
—La música de Circ és tan definitiva com no la va conèixer
Richard Wagner‾‾‾ tanmateix un pompier!

La sombra dels comparses en el sol de les taules
Moure's i projectar-se no existir:
La **VIDA** al Dinamisme

Jo protesto que això degeneri també
—Perquè ara el «domador» vol fer jocs malabars
i els cavalls amb les potes

Més m'estimo l'

i en CHA**R**L̲o̲t que s'han tornat bessons per
tal d'entrar en sèrio a la glòria del cel

(car ells són ignorants de que venim d'ahir
d'abans d'ahir de l'altre abans d'ahir
i més d'abans encara)

That man who says:
— <u>Circus</u> music is more definitive than Richard Wagner
could ever have known   nothing but a pompier!

The shade of the chorus in the sun of the boards
To move   to project   not to exist:
LIFE for Dynamism

I protest that this may also degenerate
— Because now the "lion-tamer" wants to juggle
and the horses   with their legs

My first love is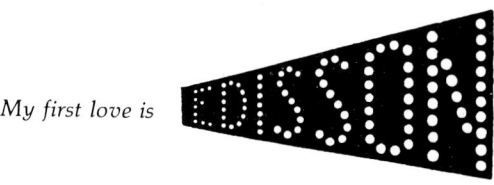

and CHAPLIN who have turned twins

to enter solemnly the glory of heaven

(for they don't know that we come from yesterday
and the day before   from the day before   the day before
        and still further before)

L'Esfera del rellotge a les <u>DOTZE</u> fecunda les hores
que vindran   que són :

una	dues	tres	quatre
cinc	sis	set	vuit
nou	deu	onze	

i després el

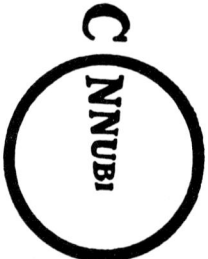

—i així seré immortal perquè d'aquí ha nascut el meu
JO dins el **TOT**

The   Orb   of   the   clock   at   TWELVE   spawns   the   hours
to come   which are:

one	*two*	*three*	*four*
five	*six*	*seven*	*eight*
nine	*ten*	*eleven*	

and after

— and so I will be immortal as from now has been born
my I in the ALL

NADAL

A Emili Badiella

Sento el fred de la nit
                    i la simbomba fosca.
Així el grup d'homes joves que ara passa cantant.
Sento el carro dels apis
                    que l'empedrat recolza
i els altres qui l'avencen, tots d'adreça al mercat.

Els de casa   a la cuina
                            prop del braser que crema
amb el gas tot encès han enllestit el gall.
Ara esguardo la lluna, que m'apar lluna plena;
i ells recullen les plomes,
                            i ja enyoren demà.

Demà posats a taula oblidarem els pobres
—i tan pobres com som—
                            Jesús ja serà nat.
Ens mirarà un moment a l'hora de les postres
i després de mirar-nos   arrencarà a plorar.

CHRISTMAS

For Emili Badiella

I feel the cold of night
            and hear the dark simbomba. *
As a band of young men pass by singing.
I hear the celery cart
            jar on the cobblestones
as others pass it on the way to the market.

Those at home   in the kitchen
                  by the burning stove
with the gas full on have prepared the bird.
Now I look at the moon, it seems a full moon;
and they pluck out the feathers,
                  and yearn for tomorrow.

Tomorrow at the table we will forget the poor
— so poor as we are —
                  Jesus will be born.
He will look at us for a moment with our sweets
and after looking   will start to weep.

---

*   *simbomba* — special friction drum used for accompaniment of carols.

TOT L'ENYOR DE DEMÀ

A Marià Manent

Ara que estic al llit
            malalt,
            estic força content.
—Demà m'aixecaré   potser,
i heus aquí el que m'espera :

Unes places lluentes de claror,
i unes tanques amb flors
                    sota el sol,
                    sota la lluna al vespre ;
i la noia que porta la llet
que té un capet lleuger
i duu un davantalet
            amb unes vores fetes de puntes de coixí,
            i una rialla fresca.

I encara aquell vailet que cridarà el diari,
i qui puja als tramvies
                i els baixa
                tot corrent.

I el carter
que si passa i no em deixa cap lletra m'angoixa
perquè no sé el secret
                de les altres que porta.

I també l'aeroplà
que em farà aixecar el cap
el mateix que em cridés una veu d'un terrat.

NOSTALGIA FOR TOMORROW

For Marià Manent

Now that I'm in bed
                ill,
        I'm really happy.
— I'll get up tomorrow   perhaps,
and here's what's waiting for me:

City squares brimming with clear light,
and hedgerows with flowers
                        beneath the sun,
                        beneath the moon at evening;
and the girl who brings the milk
light headed
and wearing an apron
                hemmed with pillow stitches,
                and fresh laughter.

And even the young paper boy,
who jumps on the trams
                and jumps off
                still running.

And the postman
who if he passes and leaves me no letter makes me sad
because I don't know the secret
                        of the others he carries.

And the aeroplane
which makes me raise my head
as to a voice calling from a balcony.

I les dones del barri
　　　　　matineres
qui travessen de pressa en direcció al mercat
amb sengles cistells grocs,
i retornen
　　　　　que sobreïxen les cols,
i a vegades la carn,
i d'un altre cireres vermelles.

I després l'adroguer,
que treu la torradora del cafè
　　　　　　　　: comença a rodar la maneta,
i qui crida les noies
i els hi diu : —Ja ho té tot?
I les noies somriuen
　　　　　　amb un somriure clar,
que és el baume que surt de l'esfera que ell volta.

I tota la quitxalla del veïnat
qui mourà tanta fressa perquè serà dijous
i no anirà a l'escola.

I els cavalls assenyats
　　　　　　　i els carreters dormits
sota la vela en punxa
que dansa en el seguit de les roderes.

I el vi que de tants dies no he begut.

I el pa,
　　　　posat a taula.
I l'escudella rossa,
　　　　　　fumejant.

I vosaltres　　　amics,
perquè em vindreu a veure
i ens mirarem feliços.

And the women of the neighbourhood
                    early risers
who rush to market
each with her yellow basket,
and come back
           with a cabbage peeping out,
and sometimes meat,
and red cherries from another.

And then the grocer,
who takes out the coffee grinder
                    and begins to turn the handle,
he shouts to the girls
and he says to them: 'Have you got everything?'
And the girls smile
           with a clear smile,
which is the balm which spreads from the sphere he turns.

And all the gang of kids from the locality
who'll kick up such a racket because it's Thursday
and there's no school.

And the wise horses
           and the sleeping carters
under the pointed sail cloth
which dances along in the tracks.

And the wine I have not drunk for so long.

And the bread,
           laid on the table.
And the light broth,
           piping hot.

And you   my friends,
because you'll come to see me
we'll look at each other happily.

Tot això bé m'espera
        si m'aixeco
        demà.

Si no em puc aixecar
        mai més,
heus aquí el que m'espera :

—Vosaltres restareu,
per veure el bo que és tot :
i la Vida
i la Mort.

All this awaits me
                    if I can get up
                    tomorrow.

If I can rise
          no more,
here's what's waiting:

— You will remain,
to see how good it all is:
Life and
Death.

RES NO ÉS MESQUÍ

A Josep Obiols

Res no és mesquí
ni cap hora és isarda,
ni és fosca la ventura de la nit.
I la rosada és clara
que el sol surt i s'ullprèn
i té delit del bany:
que s'emmiralla el llit de tota cosa feta.

Res no és mesquí,
i tot ric com el vi i la galta colrada.
I l'onada del mar sempre riu,
Primavera d'hivern — Primavera d'istiu.
I tot és Primavera:
i tota fulla verda eternament.

Res no és mesquí,
perquè els dies no passen;
i no arriba la mort ni si l'heu demanada.
I si l'heu demanada us dissimula un clot
perquè per tornar a néixer necessiteu morir.
I no som mai un plor
sinó un somriure fi
que es dispersa com grills de taronja.

Res no és mesquí,
perquè la cançó canta en cada bri de cosa.
—Avui, demà i ahir
s'esfullarà una rosa:
i a la verge més jove li vindrà llet al pit.

NOTHING IS PALTRY

For Josep Obiols

Nothing is paltry
nor any moment barren,
nor is night's fortune dark.
And the dew is clear
as the sun leaps out, stuns
and delights in his wash:
that mirrors the bed of all creation.

Nothing is paltry,
all is rich like wine and a flushed cheek.
And the billowed sea laughs forever a river,
Spring in winter — Spring in summer.
And everything is Spring:
and every leaf ever green.

Nothing is paltry,
for the days do not pass;
and death does not come even if called.
And if you have called he hides like a hole
for to be reborn we must first die.
And we are never grief
but a delicate smile
which opens like the lips of oranges.

Nothing is paltry
because the song sings in every flake of things.
— Today, tomorrow and yesterday
a rose will wither:
and to the youngest virgin's breast comes milk.

DIVISA

L'estel d'un esguard
i el d'una senyera,

la guerra i l'amar:
la sal de la terra.

Al llavi una flor
i l'espasa ferma.

DIVISA

A l'Alfons Maseres

Viatjar terres
        no quedar-se en cap,
amar en totes una noia verge;

creure en la guerra perquè és bo el combat,
cada ferida la sang d'un poema.

Quan Déu ens cridi poder contestar:
—tant estimava que es vessava el veire.

DIVISA

Fem l'escamot dels qui mai no reculen
i sols un bes els pot fer presoners,

fem l'escamot dels qui trenquen les reixes
i no els fa caure sinó un altre bes.

Fem l'escamot dels soldats d'avantguarda:
el primer bes que se'ns doni als primers.

DEVICE

The star of a glance
the flash of a flag.

War and love;
salt and earth.

A flower to the lips
and the sword held firm.

DEVICE

For Alfons Maseres

Travel many lands
            remain in none,
love in each a young virgin;

believe in war because it is good to struggle,
each wound the blood of a poem.

When God calls be able to answer:
— I loved so much that my cup o'er flowed.

DEVICE

We are the force that never retreats
that only a kiss can imprison,

we are the force that breaks the bars
and we only fall to another kiss.

We are the force of the advanced guard:
let the first kiss be given to the first.

CRÍTICA

A Cristòfor de Domènec

—volia enamorar l'avantguardista
amb una lampareta de butxaca

jo no veia la nitra
però veia els seus ulls

—destriava la roba   i ensenyava un cosset
de vímets d'alumini

jo veia les cireres del seu pit

—li brillaven les dents
                tot d'argent viu

però jo mossegava el seu llavi de carn.

CRITIQUE

For Cristòfor de Domènec

— *she would seduce the advanced guard*
with a little pocket lantern

I did not see the nitrate
but I saw her eyes

— *she peeled off her dress   revealed a bodice*
of aluminium strips

I saw the cherries of her breasts

— *her teeth shone*
                    like quick silver

but I bit her lips of flesh.

VENEDOR D'AMOR

A la meva muller

Venedor d'amor
porta joies fines:
la noia que vols
la noia que tries.

De tanta claror
que el mercat destria
per cada cançó
dónes una vida.

Quina vida dóns
quina altra en voldries:
jo me l'he triada
moreneta i prima.

Moreneta i prima
que sembla un palmó
—si un altre la mira
li treu morenor.

Jo l'he demanada
que fos sols per mi.
L'he comprada esclava,
la vull fer lluir.

Venedor d'amor
porta joies fines,
la noia que vols,
la noia que tries.

LOVE VENDOR

For my wife

The love vendor
brings rare jewels:
the girl you want
the girl you choose.

Such is the glitter
the market displays
for every song
you'd give a life.

For each life you give
you'd want another:
I have chosen mine
slender and dark.

Slender and dark
like the shoot of a palm
— if eyed by another
she loses her hue.

I have asked her
to be mine alone.
I bought her enslaved,
I'll make her shine.

The love vendor
brings rare jewels:
the girl you want
the girl you choose.

PASSEU PEL PORT

Passeu pel Port
   que és la festa pagana!
Ara florien els pals boles d'or
i els mariners ubriacs tots cantaven:
Verge del Carme, doneu-nos l'amor.

Verge del Carme cantava en els núvols,
a cada u bé llançava un esguard:
els mariners ubriacs la miraven
i convidaven tots els vianants.

Verge del Carme dansava una estona,
no hi ha vaixell que la guanyi en dansar;
alceu els ulls que veureu la corona
com va ruixant tot d'estrelles la mar:
la meva barca n'és plena a vessar.

Verge del Carme mostra un peu tot nu
que la sandàlia se li desprenia;
els gallarets s'omplenaven de llum...

Si jo nedava prou l'abastaria.

TAKE A WALK THROUGH THE PORT

Take a walk through the Port
                              it is a pagan feast!
Now the masts were flowering bulbs of gold
and the drunken sailors were all singing:
Virgin of Carmel, bring us love.

The Virgin of Carmel was singing in the clouds,
and to everyone she cast her eye:
the drunken sailors gazed upon her
and bought drinks for all the passers-by.

The Virgin of Carmel danced for a while,
there's not a vessel can match her in the dance;
Lift up your eyes to see her crown
as it sprays the sea with stars:
my boat is overflowing with stars.

The Virgin of Carmel shows a foot so bare
for her sandal was slipping away;
streamers filled up with light ...

If I swam hard enough I'd reach her.

VORA MERCAT

el vigilant del meu barri
estava mig perdut per mor de l'opereta

per això és que s'ha casat
amb una noia grassa com una boia plena:

ell treu l'aigua del pou
i és ella qui gemega

vet aquí les veïnes com masteguen llur dèria

diu que s'ha mort la Rosa
qui l'hi havia de dir tan frescota com era
però ja se li veia que tenia una pena:
no féu res més de bo des de que el seu marit
                              [li tustava l'esquena
malviatge faci ell!

vet aquí les veïnes com masteguen llur dèria

vol dir que no plourà
—deixi que el que és avui ni sé com tinc la feina

UNA GITANA PRENYS
PORTA VENTURA NEGRA

vet aquí les veïnes com masteguen llur dèria.

BY THE MARKET

our local night-watchman
was half crazy for the love of operetta

that's the reason he got himself wed
to a buxom lass as bonny as a rounded buoy:

he draws water from the well
and it's she who groans

here's how the neighbours chew the rag

they say that Rosa's died
who would have thought and her so full of beans
but you could tell there was something up:
she never got over it after her husband cracked her on the back
damn the old sod!

here's how the neighbours chew the rag

you mean it won't rain?
— don't say that, as for today I don't know where to start.

A GYPSY WITH CHILD
BRINGS BAD LUCK

here's how the neighbours chew the rag.

SI JO FOS PESCADOR

Si jo fos pescador pescaria l'aurora,
si jo fos caçador atraparia el sol;
si fos lladre d'amor m'obririen les portes,
si fos bandit millor
                    que vindria tot sol:

—els carcellers del món no em sabrien mai l'ombra,
si fos lladre i bandit no em sabrien el vol.

Si tingués un vaixell m'enduria les noies,
si volien tornar deixarien llurs cors:

i en faria fanals
                    per a prendre'n de nous.

IF I WERE A FISHERMAN

If I were a fisherman I'd fish for the dawn,
if I were a hunter I'd chase for the sun;
if I were a love-thief they'd open the doors,
if I were a bandit even better
                              I'd go all alone:

— the jailers of this world would not catch my shadow,
if I were a thief and a bandit they would not know my flight.

If I had a boat I'd capture the girls,
if they'd want to go home they'd leave their hearts:

and I'd fan up their flames
                        to steal even more.

DEU-ME UNA SANTA

A Joaquim Horta

Deu-me una santa, enc que no sigui al dogma,
a qui pugui pregar: *Jo pecador d'amor;*
deu-me una santa que hagi estimat força,
que per pregar-li calgui un bes i una cançó.

La santa aquella que, en donar almoina,
si els seus ulls et ferien t'embraçava el coll,
i era el seu tast com la més fina noia
i al coixí del seu pit hom havia el son dolç.

Aquella santa sempre bella mossa;
no havia mendicant que no li fos devot:
era tan clara, blanca, fresca i jove
com nata de primala i com un veire nou.

Jo hi aniria de matí, en 'quella hora
en què deixo l'amiga abans no surti el sol,
quan a l'església obririen la porta:

—duria l'estampeta arran, arran del cor.

GIVE ME A SAINT

For Joaquim Horta

Give me a saint, even one profane,
to whom I can pray, a sinner of love;
give me a saint who has loved so deeply,
whose prayers are a kiss and a song.

That saint who, when alms-giving,
if her eyes pierced you, kissed your neck,
and her taste was that of the finest girls
and on the rise of her breast were the sweetest dreams.

That saint ever a beautiful girl;
there'd be no beggar who would not make devotion:
she would be so pure, white, fresh and young
like the cream of lambs-wool, like a new glass.

I would go in the morning, when I leave
my love before the sun comes up,
when the church opens its doors:

— I would bear her image all around my heart.

DEIXARÉ LA CIUTAT

Deixaré la ciutat que em distreu de l'amor
la meva barca
el Port
i el voltàmetre encès que porto a la butxaca—

l'autòmnibus brunzent
i el més bonic ocell
que és l'avió
i temptaré la noia que ara arriba i ja em priva

li diré com la copa melangiosa és del vi
—i el meu braç del seu coll—
i veurà que ara llenço la stylo i no la cullo

i em faré el rostre pàl·lid com si fos un minyó
i diré   maliciós:
—com un pinyó és la boca que em captiva.

I WILL LEAVE THE CITY

I will leave the city for I am distracted from love
by my boat
        the Port
and the live voltametre I carry in my pocket —

the humming trolley bus
and the prettiest bird
                    which is the aeroplane
and I'll tempt the girl who now comes and refuses me

I will tell her how melancholy's cup is of wine
 — and my arm about her neck —
and she will see that I throw away my pen and don't retrieve it

and I'll make my face pale like a boy
and I'll say   maliciously:
 — What a pretty mouth ensnares me.

I EL VENT DEIXAVA

i el vent deixava dintre la rosella
granets de blat com espurnes de sol
—només per dir com és la boca d'Ella:

com la neu rosa als pics

                quan surt el sol.

SOTA EL MEU LLAVI EL SEU

Sota el meu llavi el seu, com el foc i la brasa,
la seda dels seus rulls com el pecat més dolç
—i l'espatlla ben nua

              ben blanca

l'ombra corba

          incitant

              de l'esguard:

encara un altre bes

              un altre

                  un altre

—quin perfum de magnòlia el seu pit odorant!

AND THE WIND LEFT

And the wind left in the poppy
grains of wheat like flakes of sun
— only to show how sweet is Her mouth:

like the rose-snow on the peaks
                    when the sun rises.

UNDER MY LIPS, HERS

Under my lips, hers, like fire on embers,
the silk of her locks like the sweetest sin
— and her back so bare
                    all white

the curving shadow
                inciting
                        glances:

still another kiss
                and another
                        and another

— perfume of magnolia her scented breasts!

PERQUÈ ÉS ALTA I ESVELTA

Perquè és alta i esvelta
tota es sap estremir.
Si els cabells li penjaven
com el fruit del raïm
pels clotets de la sina
s'hi perdien gotims.

—Més avall si arribaven
floria l'omelic.

SINCE SHE IS TALL AND FINE

Since she is tall and fine
she knows truly how to thrill.
If her hair hung down
like the fruit of the vine
the grapes would be lost
between her breasts!

— If they reached further down
her navel would burst into flower.

I QUAN CONFIATS ELS ARBRES

i quan confiats els arbres es vesteixen
ignoren els seus ulls
nit   dia   sol   estelada plena

i les rodes de la fortuna de la seva sina

i el misteri de la rosa vermella dels seus colzes

ignoren el seu ventre
                   damunt la cripta ufana
                   que flameja el seu cos

vas de l'amor
           llet i mel en son clos
                      flor d'atzabeja:

—quan confiats els arbres es vesteixen
    Ella és la Primavera

AND WHEN THE CONFIDING TREES

And when the confiding trees are clothed
they do not know her eyes
night   day   sun   starfilled sky

and the wheels of fortune of her breast

and the mystery of the red roses of her arms

they do not know her belly
                           upon the luxurious crypt
                           that fires her body

cup of love
          milk and honey in her close
                       flower of jet:

— when the confiding trees are clothed
          She is the Spring

SI ANESSIS LLUNY

Si anessis lluny
              tan lluny que no et sabés
tampoc ningú sabria el meu destí,
cap altre llavi no em tindria pres
però amb el teu nom faria el meu camí.

Un ram de noies no em fóra conhort
ni la cançó sota el dring de la copa,
vaixells de guerra vinguessin al Port
prou hi aniria, mariner de popa.

Si jo posava la bandera al pal
i era molt alta, t'hi veuria a dalt.

IF YOU WENT AWAY

If you went away
                    too far for me to know you
no-one would know my fate either,
no other lips would hold me captive
but with your name I would make my way.

No bouquet of girls could bring me comfort
nor the song beneath the ringing glass,
if warships came to port
I'd surely be there, sailor on the poop.

If I placed the standard on the mast
and it was very high, I would see you, up there.

NOCTURN PER A ACORDIÓ

A Josep Aragay

Heus aquí : jo he guardat fusta al moll.
(Vosaltres no sabeu
què és
guardar fusta al moll :
però jo he vist la pluja
a barrals
sobre els bots,
i dessota els taulons arraulir-se el preu fet de l'angoixa ;
sota els flandes
i els melis,
sota els cedres sagrats.

Quan els mossos d'esquadra espiaven la nit
i la volta del cel era una foradada
sense llums als vagons :
i he fet un foc d'estelles dins la gola del llop.

Vosaltres no sabeu
què és
guardar fusta al moll :
però totes les mans de tots els trinxeraires
com una farandola
feien un jurament al redós del meu foc.
I era com un miracle
que estirava les mans que eren balbes.

I en la boira es perdia el trepig.

[72]

NOCTURN FOR ACCORDION

For Josep Aragay

Now then: I've watched wood on the wharf.
(You don't know
                    what it is
                              to watch wood on the wharf:
but I've seen the rain
in buckets
drenching the boats,
and the coin of anguish shivering beneath the timber;
beneath the flanders
and the pinewood,
beneath the sacred cedars.

When the armed squaddies spied on the night
and the vault of the sky was a tunnel
without the flare of carriages:
I have made a fire of shards in the black throat of the wolf.

You don't know
                    what it is
                              to watch wood on the wharf:
but all the hands of all the street kids
met like a farandola*
to swear an oath in the ring of my fire.
And it was like a miracle
drawing out their stiff numb hands.

And in the fog each step was lost.

---

*   *farandola* — a Catalan/Provençal folk-dance

Vosaltres no sabeu
               què és
                    guardar fustes al moll.
Ni sabeu l'oració dels fanals dels vaixells
—que són de tants colors
com la mar sota el sol:
que no li calen veles.

You don't know
        what it is
               to watch the wood on the wharf.
Neither do you know the prayer of the ships' lights
— which are so many colours
like the sea beneath the sun:
which needs no sails.

L'OFICI QUE MÉS M'AGRADA

A Jordi López-Batllori

Hi ha oficis que són bons perquè són de bon viure,
mireu   l'ésser fuster:
—serra que serraràs
              i els taulons fan a miques,
i de cada suada deu finestres ja han tret.
Gronxada d'encenalls, et munten una taula;
si ho vols, d'una nouera te'n faran un cobert.
I caminen de pla—
damunt les serradures de color de mantega.

I els manyans   oh, els manyans!
De picar mai no es cansen:
pica que picaràs i s'embruten els dits;
però fan unes reixes i un balcons que m'encanten
i els galls de les teulades
que vigilen de nits.
I són homes cepats
com els qui més treballin.

¿I al dic? Oh, els calafats!
Tot el Port se n'enjoia
              car piquen amb ressò
i es diu si neix un peix a cada cop que donen
—un peix cua daurada, blau d'escata pertot.
Penjats de la coberta, tot el vaixell enronden:
veiéssiu les gavines
              com els duen claror.

THE JOB I LIKE BEST

There are some jobs which are good because they give you a good living,
for example   to be a carpenter:
— they saw and saw away
                        and make boards bit by bit,
and for every browful of sweat ten windows they've made.
Swinging with shavings, they'll fix you up a table;
if you want, they'll make you a shed from a walnut tree.
And thy walk level —
on the butter-coloured sawdust.

And the blacksmiths   oh, the blacksmiths!
They never tire of hammering:
they bang and bang away, they stain their fingers;
but they make railings and balconies which enchant me
and weather cocks
which keep guard at night.
They are strapping lads
like those who really graft.

And on the docks? Oh, the boilermakers!
All the port enjoys them,
                        because their banging resounds
and they say a fish is born for each blow they make
— a fish with a golden tail, blue scaled all over.
Hanging from the deck, they circle the whole ship;
if you could see the seagulls
                        how they bring them light.

[77]

I encara hi ha un ofici
que és ofici de festa   el pintor de parets:
si no canten abans, no et fan una sanefa,
si la cançó és molt bella deixen el pis més fresc:
un pis que hom veu al sostre
que el feien i cantaven:
tots porten bata llarga
             de colors a pleret.

I encara més
si us deia l'ofici de paleta:
                    de paleta que en sap
                    i basteix aixoplucs.
El mateix fan un porxo com una xemeneia
—si ho volen
          sense escales
                pugen al capdamunt;
fan també balconades que hom veu la mar de lluny
—els finestrals que esguarden tota la serralada,
i els capitells
          i els sòcols
             i les voltes de punt.
Van en cos de camisa com gent desenfeinada!
Oh, les cases que aixequen d'un tancar i obrir d'ulls!

And there's still a job
which is a holiday job   the house painter:
if they don't sing first, they won't paint a frieze,
if the song is beautiful they leave the flat fresher:
a flat where you can see from the ceiling
that they were painting and singing:
they all wear long white coats
                              splattered with colour.

And there's more
did I tell you of the bricklayer's job?
                              a bricky who knows his trade
                              and   builds   shelters.
They build a porch as easy as a chimney
— if they want
                without ladders
                              they get to the top;
they also make balconies where you can see the far away sea
— the windows which look on the whole Sierra
and the capitals
                and the plinths
                              and the pointed arches.
They go around in shirt sleeves like the unemployed!
Oh, the houses they put up in a trice!

PROVERBI

Així la rosa enduta pel torrent,
així l'espurna de mimosa al vent,
la teva vida, sota el firmament.

EL BELL ASSOLIMENT

a Na Teresa Carner

He conegut l'amic en el temps de l'angoixa
i d'això el goig que en ve.
No he conegut l'amiga:
he conegut l'esposa, que és florir de roser.

La mare he coneguda qui fent randa de penes
ens ha aconseguit grans;
i un lleu record del pare
qui —cercant, viatger, la Fortuna— em deixava en tresor
[un germà.

Darrerament encara, un tros de mi mateix, o meravella!
com jo d'altri só un tros:
la joliua filleta,
a qui amb cançons adormo i amb deures vetllo el son.

PROVERB

As the rose swept off by the torrent,
as the flash of mimosa in the wind,
your life, under the firmament.

BEAUTIFUL UNDERSTANDING

For Teresa Carner

I've known a friend in times of anguish
and the joy this brings.
I have known no lover:
I've known a wife, a rose in flower.

I've known a mother   who embroidering pain
has reared us;
and the slight memory of a father
who — a traveller for Fortune — left me a treasure, a brother.

Still later, a part of myself, what a marvel!
just as I am part of others:
the joyful daughter
who I sing to sleep and watch over with care.

MISSENYORA LA MORT,

ha volgut visitar-me
dins les quatre parets de ma cambra
tancada.
Vestia-la una túnica vermella,
i sense soroll d'ossos s'arrossegava
impúdica en son pler.

Missenyora la Mort,
tenia els ulls d'instant.
L'instant que pot occir-me
i pot enamorar-me:
perquè sóc delitós de calenta fretura.
Son rostre fit al meu.
Pro jo ja l'esguardava
perquè s'avergonyís de ses passions,
car m'era el patiment per ma obra
d'esperit.

Missenyora la Mort
m'ha fet una ganyota de menyspreu,
i mercè d'esvair-se
de les quatre parets.

MILADY DEATH,

would visit me
in the four walls of my room
entombed.
She wore a scarlet tunic,
and slipped around
no sound of bone
shameless in her pleasure.

Milady Death
had a quick eye.
The quickness that could kill me
seduces me:
for I delight in the fever of need.
Her face fixed on mine.
But I beguiled her
with the shame of her passions,
for the pain they brought
to the labour of my soul.

Milady Death
has grimaced with disdain,
and graced me by her fading
from the four walls.